SUDDEN
LOSS
OF
DIGNITY

SUDDEN
LOSS
OF
DIGNITY

GARY SOTO

STEPHEN F. AUSTIN STATE UNIVERSITY PRESS
NACOGDOCHES ★ TX

ACKNOWLEDGEMENTS

Many of these poems have appeared in the following magazines: *American Poetry Review, Askew, Green Mountain Review, Grey Magazine, Hubbub, Huizache, Miramar, New Letters, Notre Dame Review, The Packing House Review, Ploughshares, Poetry International, Redivider, Rhino,* and *Spillway.*

The poet wishes to thank Christopher Buckley for his editorial comments—on this book as well as previous ones.

LIBRARY OF CONGRESS IN PUBLICATION DATA
Soto, Gary
    Sudden Loss of Dignity / Gary Soto
    ISBN: 978-1-62288-005-8

1. Life — Aging — United States — Poetry. 3. Title.

Book and cover design: Laura Davis
Cover Art: "Peace and Blessings," DeLoss McGraw

Manufactured in the United States of America

Stephen F. Austin State University Press
P.O. Box 13007 SFA Station
Nacogdoches, TX 75962
sfasu.edu/sfapress
sfapress@sfasu.edu

Distributed by Texas A&M University Consortium
www.tamupress.com

This book is for David Ruenzel.

CONTENTS

One

One

A CHANGED MAN

Today I'm not going to eat anything
That had a mother. I'll pet the porcupine
And place a squirrel on my knee—
I have a joke or two to tell.

The animal kingdom includes the snail,
Intrepid sailor, but not the button-sized tick
Pulled from my cat's scruff. I'm ecstatic
At sighting a chickadee perched on the doghouse.
Kangaroo, hop to it.

Perhaps it's not too late to learn the musical saw
Or to play the flute—let's see snakes rise
From the hearts of corrupt men.
I could lower my eye to a microscope
And discover the Spanish Armada of all germs—
Amigos, it's not too late to learn.

Retired, I've claimed territorial rights
Of my backyard. The sprinkler swings
A faint rainbow over a fertilized lawn.
The bees nose the frangipani. Flowery trees
Scent the air around my no-longer-mortgaged house.
And look! An apple pie cools on the windowsill.

For me, it's no longer dog-eat-dog.
I'm in my lounge chair, sweetened tea in my paw.
I look skyward where geese,
Grouped for survival, honk and fly past,
Still at work, still far from home.
I intend to reset the fallen nest
In the branches, and through those branches
Admire the sun's climb to stardom.

Juggling a Galaxy of Fruit

First oranges,
Then apples and oranges,
A grapefruit if you can handle this clownish act,
You the retiree with a new hobby.

Why not the banana—
Why not the bloodshot tomato—
Why not a carrot to better your eyes—
The princely pomegranate without a kingdom?

You venture from the kitchen to the bedroom—
Wife on the bed with a novel that plods like a camel,
She with snacks to feed herself
On her dry journey.

What now?
The wife asks, not looking up.
You add to the whirl those cherries in her palm,
Then the half shells of pistachios,
The raisin on her collar—
Ah, cereal from breakfast.

Then she, your wife with rings inside her like a tree,
Rolls from her stomach and finally looks up
At that galaxy you're juggling.
What the heck, *hombre*!

Her painted toes are red as berries,
Her squinting eyes almond,
Her belly a pear.
Oh, it's just me, I'm juggling.

No, she screams, no, no!
You toss her into this mix,
The peach of sweetness,
No, the sugar rush of plum and watermelon.
She's dizzy in this big spin,
This marriage that's mostly seed and juice.

You're a man with a hobby.
You're mixing a new sort of granola,
Little of this, a little of that,
Salt from your brow, a pinch of love
Every time she comes around.

A Saturday Project

I received Cs in wood and metal shop,
Was never handy—god, the memory of a coat hanger
Worked down the gagging bathroom sink!
Everything I touch, this Allen wrench for instance,
These clamps noisy as cymbals, the toy hammer
That comes with the kit, has been misused.
Still, my wife has asked for help: Can you handle this?
I hitch up my pants and give it a try...
An hour later the IKEA bookshelf is modern sculpture,
Angled and twisted when I let go.

I spit an angry nail, taste of work not done right.
I open a beer, for I need to dull the memory.
From the picture window,
Square after all these years of marriage,
I watch the clouds in a tidy row slide eastward.
Real nice, I think. I sip my unearned brew.

Then I see: a tattered cloud
Chugging behind and getting thinner,
Gasping to keep up...
The kind I would build at that workstation
Where clouds are blown up, filled with rain,
Mine a clunker, with its lightning long gone.

ON SCHEDULE

To be born in 1899,
As Borges was,
Or born in 1878
As Jack London was,
Or brought into the light in 1847
As Thomas Edison was...
All great men now
With rocks on their chests,
The sea far away.

I'm part hourglass,
Having eaten at least a minute
Of childhood sand.
I'm an occasional sundial,
Having for six decades
Thrown out a shadow.
The god on the Aztec calendar
Has stuck its tongue out at me,
And I tap my watch
To keep it plugging along.

The river flows
And, as such, is a clock,
As are the clouds
With their brisk oars,
The petals of the tulip
With its own timetable—
It will attract the bee
And the bee will do its work.
And look! The moon
Is one day faint,
The other day milky white.

And the candle, I see,
Sputters wax down one side…

To be born a Medici,
Gold coins under the mattress,
Or drunken Pope Clement
With brats at his feet,
Or Genghis Kahn,
An enemy's beard
Crocheted into slippers…
All great men,
All builders and doers
Now with boulders
Holding down their bones,
The sea far away,
The herds of us humans
Still clashing above.

To be born in 1952,
April if scholars care to know.
I'm no doer,
No builder, no statesman
With his hand over his heart
Reciting the party line.
True, I've fathered,
I've built a house
With three windows,
Each for the people
I love best. But at least
No brick has been purchased
In my honor
And plugged into the wall
Of a theater—I'm no one
Other than an old gent

Tying his shoe laces
At the end of the corner,
A cricket of pain in his knee.
I'll take my calendars
To the sea, and toss them
Leaf by leaf, into rough waves.
I'll fill my hourglass
—a second here, a minute there—
As the sand whips up,
And I taste the salt
Of every living thing.

BLEMISH

She didn't have much to say to me
Young woman by the second-rate statue of David
In the foyer of a concert hall
Veined marble climbed the walls
And the echoes were like storm troopers

Oh she's polished she said
Her appraisal of the mezzo-soprano
She sipped her Chablis
And caught me staring

She wore a scar near her mouth
A little checkmark from school
When she turned
The blemish disappeared from view

That's Ok I thought
In heels she was taller than me
Her hair like rain from a roof
Her necklace drops of dark blood

The second-rate David
Stood behind her
And we drank our drinks
When the house lights blinked
The concert goers
Squeezed through the door
Each of us with our own scars
The mezzo-soprano screaming
In the second half
For all we had suffered

To Keep Going

I'm going to do small things,
Like bring a spoonful of water to my potted cactus.
I may deface a sentence in my journal.
I may sweep up all my misplaced commas
And boomerang them into the sea.
I may ball up a sheet of letterhead
And nibble an eraser,
A writer's snack between paragraphs.
And the paperclip?
I'll twist that plated wire until it hollers.

How far should I go?
I could dress like a penguin
And appear unannounced in Sweden,
Medals on my chest from battles
With the Spanish subjunctive?

I could bring a sponge to England
And wipe the face of Dr. Johnson's tombstone?
But let rain and the rain's acid do that janitorial work.

My ambition...
To lift a spoonful of water to my mouth,
Good ole' medicine, for the cactus can survive
On sunshine. The penguin could go it alone,
Wings at his side, and every tombstone,
A tablet of sorrow, could sink slowly in the ground.
I have to think of myself, age sixty-one,
And that journal cluttered with commas,
The dark-hearted period, the swashbuckling dash.
I'll ride the waves of the ampersand,
Arm myself to the teeth with brackets,

Or maybe go alone like the penguin,
Head down, wings at my side,
Footsteps lost in the frost of a blank white page.
A domain that required a passport.
I have the strength to scratch a lottery ticket
Twice a week. But I can't get out of the chair
Or absorb rumors from across the room.
My bones have forgotten their music.
My left hand holds hands with the right—
Is this my only friendship?

My sigh moves the page of a thin book.
My sneeze alters the position of the dead fly on the sill.
Where is the god that matters?
Where are the Canadian geese that darkened
My childhood sky? God in the shape
Of a plastic cross, wind-slick bird
Refusing to fly south, or even me
In a reupholstered chair...
I've seen too much of the world
To lift a finger.

BODY PARTS

My legs, wire coat hangers twisted in anger,
My head, a radish with a single tear,
My arms, limbs with empty nests,
My stomach, a satchel of two cats headed for the river.

At this age, I admit my fear—
Will I push a shopping cart of recycled cans and bottles,
Me at the reins of a failed wagon train?
Will I become homeless and ghost the street,
The soles of my shoes lashing pitifully at the sidewalk?
I have no strength. My hair once bounced
When I frolicked and now lays against my scalp,
Each sweaty follicle thinking, Am I next?

I eat a potato chip. I eat a carrot.
My jaws go up and down, the most purposeful
Action I'll see today. And to think I was a playground kid
Rounding the bases from morning to dusk.
How grass sprouted in my hair.
How my neck produced its own Ganges.
And what about the trees I climbed,
The wind whistling "Yankee Doodle" in my splayed ears?
How I remember the old folks in their gardens.
They lived for tomatoes and chilies,
And the brain of all veggies, the cauliflower.
When they bent over, they grunted from exertion.
When they moved a hose into the furrows,
They propped their hands on their hips
And watched them fill—the ants were living
In Biblical times,
Each one scrambling for higher ground.
Old age was another country.

THE WRONG ANSWERS
For Martin Amis

What is your novel about?
The nightly host asked in a small room
Strangled with electrical cords.
I had been living on yawns
For the last fifteen minutes,
Yawns and the breeze from fanning my novel.
I answered: It's about 125 thousand words,
Three hundred pages, one death,
A cornfield gone wild.
Tomorrow I'm at a Barnes & Noble in Wichita.

Out the door, I clutched my book
And realized it's a long way to Kansas—
No, it's just right there. A tornado
Spun its tail in the distance
And was headed my way,
Voices inside howling
The wrong answers.

DR. FREUD, PLEASE

It was a short night
Down a long hallway
Where at the end a polar bear
Was drinking from the toilet.
The bear looked up, beads on his chin.
He stood tall as a white Christmas tree
And gave me, well, a bear hug.

O Jesus, O Buddha, my wife says,
Her newspaper slapped open to the business section—
Our mutual funds are down, will remain down.
Why can't you have nice dreams?
She asks, and turns the page.

I dress first putting on my socks,
Then my shirt—I need good habits.
I eat a bowl of cereal sugared by half a banana.
I trace my palm—the lifeline
Is far too deep for what I have to do.

I look out the window: no bear,
Just rain like a long silver sleeve
Running in the streets. And, look,
A neighbor, a plastic bag
Gloved over his hand, picks up steaming dog turd.
Is this it? We end our days following
A Chihuahua on a short leash?

Dr. Freud, where is the bear in real life?
Where is the comb whittled from a whale's tooth?
The cheetah that runs daylight ragged,
The cobra with a snap judgment?

Where is the blood spilled in honor
Of the women we love, or sort of like?
My armada? My annexed territory?
A bar of unsinkable soap
In a steamy bath is no answer.

Dr. Freud consider my cat, a declawed sissy boy
Who spends his days licking his paws.
True, fangs gleam in his skull.
I possess fangs of my own,
But our meals are bloodless,
Almost vegan. I drink from a cup,
He drinks from a bowl—what's the difference?
And note this, dear dead doctor:
When we sleep, our legs twitch,
And not from the hunt
But from trying to run away.

BLAME

From this cherry pit, an orchard
And bees like bells.

From this leather,
A shoe and the sole's imprint on wet grass—
The blades spring back when we're gone.

From this feather,
A tickler to start us laughing.

From the judge's gavel,
Three strikes for the barefoot sailor.

Enough of my roster—
Cherry pit, shoe, feather, and judge's gavel.
Love, you've had a bad dream
And I was in that dream.
I wasn't to blame.
I was asleep in the other bedroom,
Or at least my eyes were closed,
Pupils like fists opening and closing.

For breakfast,
I hammer a pomegranate against the sink's edge,
And tear it open—juice on my fingers,
My face mirrored in those radiant seeds.
I temporarily died
For that fruit was my heart,
Was a nightcap before bed,
Was a husk left on the nightstand.

I was the center of a bad dream,
And as we sleep in different beds,
I wasn't even there.

First Impressions

On new grass, you're asked to tread lightly—
A trail of tiptoeing footsteps,
Landmarks for the pilgrim ant,
The weight of your presence
In the nutritious sun.

On new grass
You can make an impression,
Unlike when you meet a scholar
Smarter by at least a hundred books
And three dead languages,
Smarter in ironed clothes, breath like blossoms,
And sunglasses on top of her post-doctoral head.
She's Venus rising from the sea, but with a Ph.D.
You gulp, you swallow yet another gulp.
You say, scratching the elbow patches on your Harris Tweed,
"Moby Dick frolicked in the Seven Seas…"
At that, you squeeze your eyes shut.
If only you could jump into the polluted Aegean Sea.

She who knows, she who has a sigh for your effort,
Pulls down her sunglasses to dim your presence.
You're a little old man,
Shoelaces losing their grip,
Elbow patches hanging like scabs.
You can make an impression on grass,
Walk across it with the stature of a man with a small tool,
And dare to look back at the ants fitting nicely
Into your shoeprints. They march away,
Grass springing back, the dew simmering under the sun,
Not a single blade crushed
By knowledge.

BIBLICAL TIMES

A bush catches fire.
Locusts gum up the jars of honey.
A pair of sandals floats away from the ark.
Seas split, nations divide.
People multiply
And the dead know their place.

Face down, a body rides the Nile.
A date falls from a tree,
And flies stir—
There's so much to devour,
So much to fatten on.

With nightfall, stars roll like stones,
Wind flaps in the palm trees,
And a dog couples with the rabbit—
Sodomy in all ports of call.

This morning a camel chews its cud,
The humps on his back are full and ready.
You're the ignorant pilgrim
Who partnered with the snake,
Who wiggled to Delilah's tambourine,
Who provided change at the Temple,
Who plunged a knife
Into one brother,
Then another brother,
Just to be sure.

Born between wars,
You look for signs.
You rub salt in your wound—

A lesson in pain.
You lap water squeezed from a stone
And speak to a lone sheep
And his devilish cousin
The goat.

You mount a camel.
Call me Lord, you say,
Your neck once nearly wrung by a noose,
But that chapter didn't make the big book.
When you swat the camel's flank,
It begins to clop off—
Flies on its eyelashes,
A few on your face.
Turds tumble from the camel,
A trail for the return...

Flies whisper into the camel's ear.
A snake stiffens into a cane,
And the sun burns on the horizon.
Night, the stars are dead wrong—
Where you're headed no one speaks
Of salvation.

EYESIGHT AT FIFTY-NINE

It must have been easier
To usher the proverbial camel
Through the eye of a needle
Than this lick of thread.
Earlier, in spitting rain,
I was sidetracked by one crazy on a Berkeley corner,
And then tried to reason with the ATM machine—
Please, no receipts, no auto loans,
Just three clean twenties.

Now I struggle with needle and thread,
Lifeline from a nearly bald, wooden spool.
I can't see, I can't hear,
But my legs, thin as breadsticks,
Allow me to promenade around the block—
How often I am slowed by the elastic struggle
Of chewing gum on the soles of my shoes!

What's next?
My teeth smiling in a jam jar?
A toupee that blends nicely with the hair in my ears?
Large-print novels with pages the size of eye charts?
Be brave, I tell myself. For Jesus-Crippled-Christ,
Remember the babes who chased you around a small table!

Thus, I am mending a gym sock,
Or would if I could thread this needle.
The dehydrated camel went through nicely
And this thread, moistened by the tears
Of frustration on my cheek,
Stands soldierly straight,
But, like me, slowly grows limp.

MUSIC & DANCE

The black brother said, I know we're different
Colors, but can we talk? A dead cigarette
In his mouth, one eye closed as if he were taking aim,
And what was he but a Santa with a plastic bag
Of aluminum cans over his shoulder. He shifted
The bag and made a poor person's music.
Sorry, friend, I said, and skipped by him,
A melody in my own pocket—quarters and dimes,
A tambourine of better living. I was off to the store
For bread and peanut butter, maybe apricot jam,
A sugar rush to excite me for the longest day of the year.
I don't eat much, I don't expect much.
If you showed me an original Picasso
In an original frame, I would sigh, Oh, yeah, him.

I left the store with a plastic bag in my hand,
And hurried, the coins in my pockets
Again jingling, as I had sighted what I thought
Was a pigeon with a pencil in its beak.
Were birds now writing their memoirs?
I was wrong. It was a French fry,
Bird with his own daily purchase.
I then felt a pencil in my pocket,
A dull stub,
And thought if I were only Picasso on a bad day
I could draw my face
And staple it to a telephone pole—
Have you seen this poet? His books are remaindered
In every other bookstore. Then I looked up: the brother
Was dancing on a mighty pile of aluminum cans,
The cigarette in his mouth now fired up,
Arms waving over his head,
The jubilee of ordinary treasure.

AN AFTERNOON AT THE RIVER

Before long,
Fish on our lines swung toward the bank,
One spooked eye looking at me
Saying, OK, feed the masses.

The masses were three divorced men
Scratching their ankles.
We had trekked through a field,
Watched a hawk shadow like an ominous blade,
Rabbits and gophers,
Crickets in their armor,
Ants with jaws that could open flesh
And crawl in...

We hiked from the city,
But the city was with us—
Candy wrappers like pale flowers caught in the brush,
A car fender, a shopping cart without wheels,
Juice boxes, a child's mattress.
We washed our hands in that riverbank.
They came out clean,
Drops like contact lenses on our fingertips.

I extracted from the river
A trout that had been sad all its slick life,
Mouth pulled down, gills like a slash,
The rainbow dying on its sides.

Little trouble when the hook was pulled,
Not a flinch from that fish
Though eggs spilled from its body,
Eggs I shook onto the water for more of the same

Six months hence.
The river flowed
With its haul of light and fish eggs,
And left three men huddled in plaid,
Their own rainbows dying.

AMBITION

I planted thirty-three tulips
In honor of my teeth
And swept the drive
So my limp might enjoy a workout.
I presented my face
To a mug of hot chocolate,
And followed the ant's folly
On the doily of my armchair.
When I blew on this trooper,
He clung to the threads
For dear life. He knew famine,
He knew poisonous canisters,
He knew the shadow
Of an oily thumb. What a survivor,
This little guy with a tight torso.

It was raining, it was cold,
And I had nothing to do
But ponder my body,
Satchel of flesh, radish for a brain—
I was a glutton last night.
I had to laugh at the ant,
Stubborn creature with antennae
Swiveling like radar. I had to laugh
As I appraised the row
Of pens in my shirt pocket,
Little batons of prevarication.
I sipped hot chocolate.
I thought, Yes, I planted blueberries
And blackberries, the most natural
Inks in the wild. With other
Old men, I stared into holes

Where hardhats gabbed.
Having heard enough of
The world, I undid
And pocketed my earpiece.
Retired, I presently walk in circles
Of mild satisfaction
And will stop to pet
A dog's head. I patrol sidewalks
For litter, and bending down
Fart at my saintly effort?
I eat twice a day,
Low-salt grains mostly,
And think of earth's insatiable appetite,
How it swallows our bones,
The marrow sucked
And tasteless in the end.

DEER FROM THE HILLS

As clear as day
My wife saw a deer in our front-yard tomato patch,
Three miles from what we can call country.

As clear as day
I saw her at the stove,
Rousting sliced onions among trooping potatoes.
She wiggled the pan,
Blue sparks like commas,
Smoke engineered from four strips of bacon.

I beheld a woman in panties and a bluish t-shirt,
Her breasts rumbling,
Her hip the circumference of the equator—
A starving poet was never luckier.

She put on a robe and a happy face,
And served the omelet,
Its heart still bubbling
When I parted it with a fork.
Half-finished, I wiped my mouth
And said, You know,
I saw a coyote this morning.

She looked up from her own plate,
Her eyes the soft eyes of a soft deer,
Her breasts still heaving
From her short-order work,
Fear perhaps.

Animals are coming down from the hills,
The skunk and possum, the fox and beaver,

Snakes like a pile of rope. She forked a potato.
Her eyes pleaded: please not the coyote,
Beast that would bring down a deer
For eating no more than a tomato.

AFTERNOON IN OCTOBER
For Carolyn

I once took a farm girl's hand in mine
And walked the reservoir, first one way
Then the other. I couldn't get enough,
This handholding, wisps of her hair rising
From the wind over the alfalfa fields.

We were young, we were happy.
Sunlight and a cloud
Like a sail took us somewhere.
Somewhere was a bushy area.
We lay, we got up, we lay again.
I put a length of straw in her mouth
And she put one in mine.
The cumulus cloud rowed,
A white boat with lightning in its hull.
We were young, we were in love,
We were surprised by rain.
We put out our palms and, like horses,
Lowered our faces to these drops,
Thirsty no more.

TALKING TO MYSELF

Who wants to be a hero,
Like that ant on the windowsill

Lifting a dead comrade into his jaws—
The strength, the sense of duty!

I put down a dry turkey sandwich
And watch him stagger back and forth,

His antennae rotating. Who will clamp
Me in his jaws? Who will to push a button

That propels me on a conveyor belt
Into a nice balance of yellow and blue flames?

But maybe I can live as long as Moses,
Bearded prophet sustained by manna.

If so, then surely the young would hoist me
On their shoulders and bear me away—

More bony lumber for the earth,
More gristle beneath the heartache of flowers.

Unlike Moses I survive on sandwiches, manna
Of my own making. More or less

It's all the same. Three square meals
On a plastic plate, then night, then sleep.

The sun is a bloodshot eye in the east
When I wake tired from my dreamy travels.

For a hobby, I should collect salt shakers, blue
Dutch boys and Irish lassies with corked bottoms,

Or smoke a corncob pipe on a wharf,
Shuffling light on the surface of the waves.

No, I'll keep busy with needle and thread,
And darn socks by a log fire. By that light,

I'll remember my childhood dog Blackie,
My cat Boots, my love birds that banged heads all day,

My lizard that disappeared down the bathtub drain
And emerged in Florida as an alligator.

But the ant returns, his chum in his jaws,
Lost and bewildered, antenna going haywire.

He drops his load, lowers his head to a crumb.
Be a hero! Don't abandon your friend!

But the ant needs his daily fuel
And crawls away, faithless as any of us.

Tears & Plastic

Because you couldn't remember
What was missing,
You searched your front pockets:
Cracked button,
Dimes and nickels,
A stick of Double Mint
To sweeten fifteen minutes
Of the day,
A dollar bill and keys,
Seeds so fine
That when you're dead
Red poppies will emerge
From under your fingernails.

In back pockets:
Wallet of course,
A pencil,
A receipt with many zeros,
A photocopy
Of a lost dog named Chow.

Then you find it,
A Kleenex with tears
Folded over and over,
Same tears that moistened your eyes
When in a Technicolor movie
The sailor took a breath
And went down with the ship.
You were ten then,
Body lean as an oar
And buoyed by tears.
You dabbed at the runoff

And walked blindly
From the theater.
It was 1963,
Year of a dead president.

Now, decades later,
A plastic bag ghosts
Down the littered street
And you're searching
For a Kleenex, allergies
You think, dander
From the old kitty,
Sorrow from last-night's
Out-of-date-existential play?
Or perhaps the comment
From the green student who said

Plastic will last longer than
Ten thousand years—
Use paper, you dummies.

You have to wonder.
Plastic or tears?
Which remains longer?
Tears, you argue.
At each birth babies
With fists closed
And eyes pinched
Bawl before anything's really wrong.

THE MARRIED LIFE OF ONE COUPLE WE KNOW

God knows I've scrubbed plates,
And washed the family cars,
Herded leaves into biodegradable bags,
Brought in buckets of tomatoes,
Boiled jams on front and back burners,
And produced a polluted sea of tears—
Yes, Masterpiece Theater Jane Austen revival
Forced those tears at this hour of marriage,
Now that we're both of us tucked in bed,
Our spoons licked of medicine,
And me jabbering
Through this hour-long period piece—
O the costumes, O the green Dorset landscape,
O isn't that Dame Maggie Smith,
I mean, Dame What's-Her-Name,
You know… and when you place
Your hand on mine, a sign to knock it off,
I become quiet as smoke,
Think I will in time become smoke,
Torn apart by wind, the horizon flat as a hand,
The light silvery, very silvery,
Then not at all.

No Expectations

Aided by a Nordic wind and the moon's invisible tug,
The yacht pulled away without me.
The clouds, too, departed,
And fog seeped from the wet sand.
I returned home, lit a fire,
And poked the embers with a screwdriver—
Briefly, warmth crept up my left arm.

I slept, I rose, I made coffee...
The day repeated itself—
Again, the waves rustled up strength
And the yacht was offshore in the bay,
The three-piece combo playing on the deck.
The Chinese lanterns swung brightly,
And lovers in pairs, dancing,
Struggled out of their clothes,
No, wait a minute,
They were an old married couple
Just plain fighting!

I lifted a seashell to my ear—
Even at arm's length a voice scolded,
"You bought high, sold low—fool!"
I buried the seashell in sand.

I trolled the beach.
The pulse on my wrist jumped
At the sight of a large fish
Struggling just feet from the shore—
Hammerhead shark,
Or a barracuda with a terrible headache?
With my pant cuffs rolled,

I waded into the shuffling waves,
Said, "Fishy, I will save you."

But it was no fish,
Just a board with cloth tied on one end,
A conceptual art project thrown into the sea?

I'm not pleased with myself,
I'm not pleased with equator that divides the world.
I arrived to embark when I was told,
And every yacht, boat, canoe, log, soggy board,
Everything with any salvation
Pulled away without me.

RESPONSE TIME FOR THE OLD GENT

My old cat was doing Tai Chi
By his water bowl. He's grown slow,
This white whiskered fellow,
And now only quivers his jaw at sparrows
On the lawn. His fangs are dull,
Without luster. His claws, I see, are retracted,
Hidden like the best cutlery in a drawer.
I appraise my own claws,
Nubs chewed from penny-ante concerns.
And my fangs? Never owned a set,
Never owned much in the way
Of manly armor—no ripple
Of muscle moving like trout
When I flex my biceps.

Picture window, lots of summery light…
I'm stroking my cat,
His eyes closed in pleasure,
When a young woman walks past,
Nearly naked, in shorts and a halter top.
She'll catch cold, I worry,
A poor college student stripped
Of everything she owns…
Then the phone rings.
It's a sales pitch in Spanish—
Do I want my rug cleaned by noon?
I look up at the clock: 11:25.
I hang up, fix myself a sandwich
Plied with lettuce, tomato, and a plank of cheese—
Got to live it up, right?

Nighttime, I can't sleep.
If only I could unscrew the top
Of my head and fill it
Like a planter with a pretty flower.
Then I flinch: was the college student naked?
Were the shorts really panties, the halter top a lacy bra?
My heart flutters, and my big toe throbs—
Is this action anyway connected to not seeing right?
Confused, I look at my clock: 11:25.
It's almost midnight, I mean almost noon.
I wonder if I have time to have my rug clean
If I call right now

TODAY'S MAIL

Your attention is given over
To the coupon for cleaning wall-to-wall carpets,
And the ad for a hearing aid
No bigger than a ball of wax,
The color of wax.

Visa offers a titanium credit card.
The Jacuzzi praises its three jets.
Your teeth can be whiter than a vampire's.
Roses? Jackson &Perkin's got them the color
Of a heart attack.

And what's this from the IRS?
The gray suits calling in their chips?
And look, the Rescue Mission.
Isn't that a high school chum in the photo?
His cheeks are collapsed, teeth gone,
But it's him, the class valedictorian.

Up the street,
Mail boxes soldier straight,
Some like bird houses,
Others like galvanized barns.
The mortgages are paid,
Blooms on the hollyhock brittle.
For warmth, cats sleep on the hoods
Of Volvos, their engines ticking.

The sun struggles
Between branches of a sycamore—
The mail carrier was late again,
Poor guy doing his rounds

With his eyes half-closed.
You look down at the leaf attached
To the cuff of your baggy old-man chinos.
How did it get there?
How did you arrive here scratching
An ankle in the middle
Of the road? More leaves
In the brisk air, as a car passes—
A leaf now clings to your Mr. Rogers sweater.

You think of death,
A coffin on shoulders
And the pallbearers out of step,
Like ants, you think,
Workers on the non-union clock
And ready to angle you down a lightless hole.

TRYING TO HELP

The elevator opened at the Samaritan's touch
And he disappeared upwards,
The lights above the elevator blinking two, three, four…
He was headed to the top.

When I touched the button,
The elevator never came.
I took the stairs, burger wrappers at each turn.
On fifth floor a lone pigeon, stuff built up on his beak—
Petrified tears from sobbing?

I asked: Bird, how long you been here?
He scooted backwards, warbled.
I caught him and carried him
At arm's length.

I was exhausted, eleven floors of tiny cement steps
Littered with broken condoms
And two more pigeons,
Stuff really built up on their beaks—
All three I tucked under my arm.

I nudged the roof door open.
The city lights ignited my eyes.
There was the yellow and defiled moon
And the United Nations of poor people's towels
Hanging on a line.

I brought my friends to the ledge.
My hair moved in the city wind,
Cars honked down below.
I said: Pigeons, you're free—fly!

When I clapped my hands,
These heavy bowling balls of the bird world
Rolled over the edge without protest.

I put my hand over my mouth, scared.
I watched a single feather seesaw
In the cold air, the dark eating that feather
Eleven floors below.

Before My Doctor's Appointment

Death is no more than a whiny mosquito.
Scared? Just pinch its little head off
And wipe the grime on your jeans,
Like snot.

Still, I must be cautious
And not refer to death disrespectfully.
When Dr. Fong brings down his rubber hammer,
I swing my leg knee high—
The old joint has spring after all.

When he peers down my throat,
He sees the pink of good health.
He shines a beady light into my beady eyes—
Plenty of gray matter back there, right?

He runs his hands like mice
Over my belly, and I laugh
As I remember the joke about a penguin
That visited the zoo.

I drop my pants,
And reveal the embarrassment of legs.
My dry tool he probes with a Popsicle stick,
Asshole like a small moist snail...
Doctor Fong frowns at the lint in my belly button.
He takes my blood pressure
And listens to my heart,
Trusty two-cycle engine.
He assigns blood work—
Liver like a water bottle?
Cholesterol plastered to my heart's main artery?

A paisley-patterned germ from
A public fountain?

He asks: any concerns?
Yes, my hearing in both ears,
The camel's hump rising from my shoulder,
And the trouble of staying awake
When I'm awake,
And asleep when I'm asleep.

Doctor Fong sends me from the cramped room,
Peeling off that paper from the bed
Where I sat with pants around my ankles,
And warns me about the dangers of Eggs Benedict.

When he's not looking,
I sneer at Death.
You bug flying around the bedroom,
I'll squirt antibacterial hand sanitizer in your eyes.
I'm armed with vitamin C,
Fish oil, calcium with D,
Red wine for the pipes,
And simple dry-throated fear
For the lower congress,
The gridlock of my bowels.

But fear, potent laxative,
Loosens the bowels
When two days later
Doctor Fong holds up a fistful
Of vials. He says, I'm glad you've come—
Today, blood work
From both arms.

The Year is 2020

What were the clouds but bison
Roaming the low landscape of the sky,
And what was the open tulip
But an invitation for a worker bee.
What were the frisky college kids
On a blanket but part
Of the scenery—Jesus,
Apostles of merry times,
They were packing in free fun
In a public park. All the while
My cataracts had peeled off,
Me Mr. Lonely on a splintery bench—
I had just dusted off a 99 cent bag
Of pretzels, low on salt,
High on grit.

I smacked my lips—
Was this thirst, or desire?
I was a bachelor with two hourglasses
Going at once, with nothing
More heady than a single thought:
Gotta get milk on the way home.
Milk, I thought, don't forget the milk,
And raised my face skyward—
The bison had become large breasts.

On the swings, the three-year-olds cried.
On the slide, the older kids tumbled down backwards.
Strollers glided past,
Mothers grouped under a tree.
A golden retriever galloped
Toward a sloppy tennis ball.

Although not a voyeur,
I turned to the college kids
Now off the blanket
And on the most natural of all beds—
Sweet and pliable grass.

The blood inside me turned sluggishly,
But it turned nevertheless.
I got up, spanking the bottom
Of my pants of whatever,
And saw that my zipper was down:
Another old man thing,
Forgetful, forgetful, stupidly forget…
Now what was I supposed to buy?
Oh, yeah, I remembered:
Breasts filled with low-fat milk.

Two

MILLENNIUM BRIDGE

The party girl was down,
The pink chowder of puke
Splashed in front,
Dizziness like a carnival ride,
All because of the slushy drinks
Slurped from a docked boat
On the Thames. Been there,
Done that, I thought. I stepped
Over this lassie
In tight designer jeans,
Her golden hair lifting slightly,
And on any other day
A natural beauty. I hurried
Over to the New Tate
And pushed myself
Among the pungent crowd
Where I stood in front
Of a large canvas—
The ponytailed artist with one name,
A sufferer himself of slushy drinks,
He had painted pink chowder puke.
Was that the rage, I wondered,
The theme of the new decade?
Did I have to buy the catalog
To know?
         Later, I stood
On the wobbly bridge,
My pint of Fosters
In a paper bag.
I was alone, tired,
A reasonable man
Evident in the patches

On my old, tweed coat.
The bridge swayed,
A few of the passersby swayed.
I looked into the Thames,
Far from drunk,
Far from the rage
Of summer, my youth
Miles downstream.

ONE DAY LESS

In memory of Victor Martinez

The moon was shuttered by a cloud
When I got the call that you had died,
Maybe with one hand on your heart,
The other with the woman you loved.
A brother was at your side—
Sirens went the other way.

Two days later, the grass sighed,
The moon stirred trees, and drinking friends
Hid like possums in their lit homes.
Once, you told me that ink fails us,
That the root of our plantings dies of rage,
And in time love's fractured face becomes whole—
Vic, I thought, what do you mean?

With your life in front of you,
You followed it like a hat tumbling
Down a beautifully short road.

FOOT PATH NEAR CLARE, ENGLAND

Wind shoves clouds across the sky.
Rain taps my shoulder
Like a stranger,
And I'm suddenly in a cemetery.
Headstones like ruined teeth
Tilt in the leaf-soggy ground.

I read a name—Rebecca Waller—
Age six months...
Hands like petals on her chest,
Her face blue as willow pattern china?
The year: 1749,
A year of slaughter,
Of famine,
Of ash for all the history of wind.
I read names, all babies in a row,
Days old and gripping cloth,
Sightless as moles.

More rain, then autumn sunlight
Slanting behind the chestnut trees...
My friends of Clare
And Clare's neighbor, Dedham,
I could gallop after a cloud,
Dark underneath,
And for the children that had died
Add my own lost words.

THE GOPHER

Took away the roots of my rose bush,
Took away an onion and its elegant sister, the tulip bulb.

This I discover as I walk down the porch steps
And post my hands on my hips.
It's too late for kindness
Not after how he treated my girl.
I intend to split that gopher into two,
Earthly sailor that has journeyed
To the north side of my yard,
Weedy terrain if you want to know—
A pile of lumber, sacked leaves and ivy,
The graveyard of poisoned snails,
And an old wooden bench
Where I once discussed with a squirrel
My brief relationship with money.

Wait a minute,
I veer from the subject
Of the gopher,
Bucktoothed killer of my rose bush—
Poor spinster, still standing
But by the end of the week
Her head will drop in disappointment
And her arms will discard their leafy sails.

Where's my shovel?
Where's my right glove of justice?
I'll patrol the yard
And wait for him to surface—
He's got come up for air,
Cocky sailor with slicked-back hair,

Whiskered and fearless.
Fearless as he has eaten earth
And earth's remnants,
Leaves, sprigs, barky material,
A pebble or two,
And the roots of my rose bush.
I'm serious now.
I have my shovel,
Implement of death,
And a smoke bomb—
Let him rub his eyes!
Let him sneeze,
Let him cough smoke
Through his ears!
That sailor has taken away
My rose, still upright,
With bees hugging her pistils,
Her flowers like pink tutus,
Her scent sweet.

I'll stand like a sentry
Over his hole,
Slick my own hair back,
Show him what a pair
Of fangs I possess,
The angry red in my eyes,
And the cat inside me
Waving my tail
From side to side.

Superhuman Talents

On Monday,
I balanced the national budget
On the end of my index finger.

Later, I read a book while I napped
And composed a ditty between cosmic yawns.

On Tuesday,
I righted the Leaning Tower of Pisa.
I drank coffee, cracked my knuckles
And stayed up late
Translating Szymborska.

On Wednesday,
I fell asleep in a meadow.
When I woke
With an ant trafficking my ear,
I connected the dots of the universe.

On Thursday,
I located Noah's Ark by scratching a ravine
With a bent spoon—
What was hard about that?

On Friday,
I talked the Loch Ness Monster onto a dinner plate—
Its tail alone fed a family of twelve.

On Saturday,
I brought peace to Iraq
And cleaned the Tigris River with a tennis racket—
Jumping gaily, the fish have returned.

On Sunday,
I tidied up a lost sonata by Satie,
Fellow artist dead nearly fifty years.

How do I do it? Exercise is the key.
You build up a big wind from running in circles,
But in the end give it all back
To the Big Sky.

But first Stockholm and the Nobel Prize!
I drink Dom Perignon, spoon Russian caviar,
And laugh in three languages.
On a really tall box, I accept my prize for Chemistry—
Who knew that bullshit could be turned into gold?

SCIENTIFIC READING

In these fast food times
Even the ants,
Once frail as shadows,
Are obese—how they love
The 48-ounce Big Gulp.

Right now
On the side of a littered road
They're ransacking a donut—
The hell with spotted banana peel,
Forget the apple and its bitter seeds.

A newbie carves his way out
Of that sugary house, wired.
He spurts ahead,
Little junkie, crack head,
And turns in a circle six times—
Then, with jaws clacking,
He attacks his brother's share.

ADVICE

The prophet said
Forget the year then the day
The hours when the geese go south

Forget the cow and the cow's hour before the hammer
Forget the willow leaning over a canal
Forget the spanking of a shoe's sole against the sidewalk

And above all forget your birth
Those candles leaning on a two-layer cake
The smoke like tiny nooses when you blow them out

I read a spiritual text at the kitchen table
With a herd of crumbs from a brownie on the other side
A frontier of sweetness

The prophet with a long finger said
Forget the rotation of a bike's tire
Forget the child jumping over a leaf fire
Forget the puckered face of a raisin
We're little hills he said
Bulges under the fattened earth
Dead before we have a chance to live

I can't believe this bearded fellow
I'm here to remember
For I've seen a friend
His brain like a sack of sand
Staring at a paisley carpet in the hospital

I gather up the crumbs in my palm
I expect sweetness, not this prophet who rode a camel
Not the sands he promised
Not a hellish sun crawling across the road

The geese are going south
The wind north
I'm ten and will always be ten
Dead father has been calling me home

AN ODD MOMENT

I was reading
From an old book of poetry
When the 9th grade class of Catholic girls
Began to yawn, each of them
A little bird wanting to be fed
Something other than sweet John Keats.
To save the moment,
I asked, "Ladies, what's
Your favorite dessert?"
None raised a hand.
Some moaned and reached
Into their sleeves for cell phones.
How long would this fossil go on?

Failing to reach the young,
I left the school and sat in a park
Where I befriended a small dog
With a mighty hose between his legs.
How in the hell was he born with that!
I laughed. I petted
His scruff and read his dog tag—
Stud. I lived briefly in his eyes,
In the wag of his tail.
For mineral intake, I guess,
He began to lick my hand,
Me an old salt block.

Clouds passed, birds passed.
I looked at my face in the public fountain—
Truth and beauty had passed as well.

HERO WORSHIP: ON DISCOVERING A FAMOUS FIGURE IS NOT WHAT HE CLAIMED

I could eat dust, as I am dust.
The sun rides my back, I the sundial
With a pile of unused minutes.
The clouds slide overhead, anxious to get out of town.
The trees snap, the red poppies open and close,
Wounds that bleed daily.

OK, we have no heroes,
This is what I want to say—
The Samaritans on litter patrol have gone home.

What do I do now?
I want to push a fist into the earth
And pull up a saintly bone.
I want to swat a gnat from the Dalai Lama's robe,
And kiss the hem of Mother Teresa's gown.

I'm not Buddhist, I'm not Catholic.
I'm made of flesh and, thus, meant for trouble.
Still, I like to think we have heroes pulling long ropes.
Once, I tried to save a pigeon.
I picked up the creature,
That live shuttlecock,
And placed him on a ledge—
I was tipsy on top of a San Francisco hotel,
My scalp relinquishing more hair
Into an urban wind.

O Jesus, O Buddha,
O Ganges that runs through our dirtied veins!
I tried to help this bird relearn

What he had forgotten,
He with one leg missing,
An eye half shut.

I spread the pigeon's wings like a fan
And felt all he needed was a refresher course.
I lifted him like a chalice, cried, Fly!
The bird dropped without a sound,
Other than the whisper
Of wind through his open beak,
Nine stories into the gray alley
Of oblivion.

CEMETERY OUTSIDE OF DEDHAM, ENGLAND

Thirty-plus tilting headstones,
The names washed by rain and rain's cousin, fog…
Below, candidates for resurrection,
Mary, Elizabeth, Jonas, Martin the Good…

I walk among the graves, soft as bread under foot,
And I think of a friend with specks on her lungs—
Five months, a year she is given.

Forced to live with their arms out,
The ancient oaks moan.
A blackbird calls out a warning.
A motorcycle idles at the side of the wet road—
A young man is pissing a frothy pint in the weeds.

Another Mary, another Elizabeth…
And a headstone is toppled over.
Since it's a thin stone tablet,
I turn it over—
John Bartlett, in his Father's arms,
It faintly marks the year of his death: 1724.

I'm a visitor, no, I'm an exhausted tourist.
Like a headstone, I may fall on my face.
Will rain tap my back to get up?
Will a blackbird visit my knuckles for one last peck?
Clouds over the ash-colored hill,
And the motorcycle is gone,
Its roar now whiny gnat in the distance.
The leaves stir above the graves,
But unlike the morning light
No good soul will rise.

Tax Audit Nostalgia

Pet the rabbit's foot,
Nail the horseshoe over my bed,
Stir the tea leaves at the bottom of a cup.

I'm thinking of ways out
As The Man stirs my receipts set in a pile—
The tax-deductible leather satchel,
The dinner for two in Vegas, the gas for a long-ass haul
To Bakersfield, the Mont Blanc pen.

What is it you do? The Man asks.
Not a lot, I confess in my heart,
Think that maybe I pet the rabbit's foot the wrong way,
The horseshoe fell on my head,
The tea from China was toxic.

Entertainment, I finally answer,
Then gaze down at the button on my shirt,
Barely on, a head coming off.

The Man lowers his head,
Polished bald from reluctant citizens like me.
He crunches a Lifesaver,
A little sweetness for his time with me.
He repeats, Soto, Soto…

I see myself standing behind bars
In an orange jump suit,
A cup for coffee and my lukewarm tears.
I see myself rendering
The Sistine Chapel on a cuticle,
Me suddenly the artist in cell Number Three.

The Man takes off his eyeglasses,
Leans backs and rubs his Buddha belly.
He asks, Wasn't there a pitcher named Soto—
Reliever for the Reds?

Though not a rabbit's foot,
I rub my thumb, lucky me.
He's a baseball fan, and I bear the name of a pitcher
From the 1970s when I was broke,
When I was penniless and my hair was black,
When God almighty I was on third base
Ready to steal home.

THE TELEVISION STAR NOW BANKRUPT

Designer teeth, maybe a Gucci wristwatch,
A four-hand massage on a Friday,
A basket of pears flown in from Italy,
And doves released for peace...
Oh, Jesus, the birds didn't get far
Before they were brought down
By a badass Boy Scout with a B–B gun.

The star's money was poured down a cleavage
Of a seventeen-year-old—the lawsuit ruined him.
He now lived in a condo—the shame.
He traveled economy, he rotated sour wines in his cellar,
And read scripts by a fake log fire.
The women, mermaids by the infinity pool,
Wiggled into tank tops and flopped away.

Once, a trout met him at the edge of a lake
And offered up a bubble. The star offered three tears,
But the lake was already full of sad reruns.
The trout mouthed a second set of bubbles,
Kicked a fin and shimmied away—
Was this a sign to follow?
He didn't have his camera, or a clear eye,
For he had enjoyed three tropical drinks
In less than an hour.
His brain, a dry sponge, thumped.
The trout mouthed bubbles,
Then slowly sank, like a dream.
This is how one starts, if passably good—
A television deal, a mermaid in the afternoon.

He touched his front teeth—
They were his. His Rolex? Gone,
Though a pulse ticked between
The veins on his wrist.
Wind rearranged his hair.
I could have been Richard,
He brooded, as in Richard Gere,
A little older now. He breathed in—
A poor-man's liposuction. The star,
Without a mid-day slot on television,
Shivered from the shadow
Of passing starlings,
Placed his hands like stones
In his pocket. If you start young,
You are tossed out before it's really over.
The sun, dipping into water, is something
Like an eye, red and going down, down, down.

ETERNITY AT ZAK'S CAR WASH

Set in neutral, the station wagon rolled
Between rails, was lathered and rinsed,
Blown dry by a howling siren,
Mirrors wiped of soapy tears
By a Guatemalan with a gold grille,
And finally frisked by a vacuum—
The French fries on the mats stood up
Solider straight, some quivering,
Before they flew up the hose,
Rattling toward the end of a clotted tunnel.

Graffiti in a Regional Park

On the trail,
The rock said, Shit.
The tree roared, Bite me.
The fence that had gone down read, Bitch.
I ignored these outbursts
And got comfy on the grass.

I wanted sleep, I wanted nature,
I wanted a worker bee to enter a tulip
And emerge strengthened.

Overhead a cloud stalled
And I thought of Jesus picking at slivers—
The way He was treated
Why would He want to come back?
I chewed on a stalk of grass
And prayed for lightning.

On the way back,
Every other rock said, Fuck!
Many a tree roared, Snitch!
On the trail, a spray can and two squirrels
Jabbering, high on fumes.

I wanted sleep, I wanted nature.
I wanted a saint with a big sponge to descend
From the sky and wipe out the graffiti
Like the sins of the Dark Ages.

GLOBAL WARMING

The Canadian geese have broken all rules
And have settled in Alabama.

In Florida, a gator has crossed the two-lane highway—
Note a clothesline between its teeth like dental floss.

Polar bears fling ice cubes at each other.
Clouds pass with bunched-up faces.
Daffodils come up in a snow storm.
Trees whip themselves,
S &M even in nature.

We experience hot flashes,
Or at least my wife walks
Around the house, an ostrich feather in her hair,
Her thong a rubber band aimed
At my smirk.

My cat licks the places where wounds will appear.
I scratch my palm—
Will a stigmata burst open?
Will the spools of film finally
Fall from my eyes,
My movie finally financed?

Al Gore presents a slide show—
Nobel Peace Prize for him.
Obama tightens his belt—
Gee, one for him, too.
Can't forget Kissinger, blood on his paws,
With his trophy.

The congress debates a supply of pencil sharpeners,
Their anger hot enough to inflate balloons.
We degreed citizens survive them,
Our shirts faded on our backs,
The buttons on our cuffs hanging
By a thread.

I have no problem with the Canadian geese or the gator,
Or the penguins like missionaries
Waddling up the street
In pairs.

I have no problem
With the cougar in my backyard—
Let the tomatoes drip like blood from his chops.

Time wipes its haggard face on the kitchen clock.
I know fire but not snow.
The clouds return with lightning,
With spitting hail and thunder in their bellies,
But those of us suited up in fur and flesh...
We're not coming back.

FAMILY GATHERING

From the front window
It's always Christmas Eve, 1963.
In an orderly v-shape geese aim south,
Somewhere warm
Where in leisure they can peck lice from their feathers
And poke each other in the eyes.

In his recliner, my stepfather is drunk,
And my mother is in the hallway,
Her face spooked with pinkish night cream.
My left nostril remains plugged with a cotton ball—
A cartwheel off the garage roof, if you want to know.

None of us will sing "Little Drummer Boy."
None says grace, none gets nice gifts,
Only pencils wrapped in tissue paper,
Socks we fit on our hands like boxing gloves,
And oranges with their arsenal of seeds
To spit at each other.

Christmas Eve, frost on the window…
Baby Jesus, weaned on a pickle,
Is born anew with eyes squeezed shut.

All Better Now

Summer 1958, when I thought I could make
Things better on my street. Come here,

I whistled to my dog under the chinaberry tree.
Blindly, for his eyes were cataracts of passing clouds,

Blackie lapped a dissolved aspirin from a soup spoon.
He curled up and curled up again in a grave.

The spoon went back into the kitchen drawer,
Among forks and knives, the potato peeler

That I once raked against my finger just to see.
Blood was what I saw, blood was what I was.

Early on, I tried to save others,
Like my dog, then later a kitten that fit in my shoe,

Then myself by walking through a wreath
Of Catholic incense—what happened?

Is my failure a checkmark on God's clay tablet?
Should I have had been born with a warning?

Spoon and aspirin, dog and boy—
A silent blend will stop a heart cold.

The Integrative Action of the Nervous System

Began at the kitchen table,
Stepfather with his empty shot glass,
As he repeated, *Implements* is a hard word to spell.
My cue to lift my head
From the table and begin, I-m-p-l...
Then fuck up the word so that he could rise
And stumble to the pantry for the bottle,
His hand around the neck,
Ready to tip it back.

I was introduced to that word in winter—
In the yard, two black birds dueling
With their short beaks
And weeds that could cover a grave no one visited.
An implement, I learned, could be a rolling pin
For the back of his head.

On my own, I learned that geese swung south in winter,
Back up north for spring—they flew above
Our neighborhood with their eyes filled with foreign lakes.
I learned stepfather was swinging his own rolling pin
To his head nightly, bruising parts of his brain
Through drink and repetition—
We never got beyond *implements*,
His idea of a professor's word.

I never used that word,
Or the sweet spot of the rolling pin.
The geese, I realize,
Were too dedicated to flight
To look down at the domestic slaughter.

ON MY MOTHER'S FRONT LAWN

In despair on the front lawn,
You whispered, Everyone go out for a pass…
Everyone was three little kids in eyeglasses,
One with a limp, two with noses plugged with snot.
They went long and deep
And kept running, losers at the beginning
Of a wintry day. When they ran away
The other team of prison-bound bullies pushed you,
Spat at your feet, and then disappeared.
Cold, you breathed and breathed,
And the cloud in front of you held no lightning,
Not even a spark.

Again you're on your mother's front lawn.
You've not seen her for two decades,
Your teammates even longer—
Maybe the weakling with the limp straightened out.
You assess the steam-fogged kitchen window,
Steam from the simmering soup,
Steam from your mother's anger—
She will always be mean.
You want to go inside this winter,
To say rough if not righteous things
And even the score.

You stomp your boots for heat
And walk away, hands in your pocket.
Breath slides across your cheeks,
Like smoke. On the next block
A kid plays Frisbee with his pup,
Who, you see, can't catch, can't trot.
The runt flops over his feet,

Sick and with his eyes half-closed.
The kid bends down to his buddy
And places the Frisbee in his mouth.
See, he says, you catch it like this.

THANKSGIVING DINNER

I followed a dog
As far as I could—up an alley,
Along a canal with hideous frogs,
And by a smoky hobo camp.
Wet from rain, I turned around
And went home. At home,
The orange porch light a beacon,
The TV shuffling its light, two baby brothers
With tinker toys in their gooey mouths...
Stepfather drunk in his recliner,
Mother angry over the howling noise
Of a two-speed blender—the potatoes
Were really taking a beating.
.

I was hungry, forever ten-years-old.
I stood over the floor furnace,
Heat rolling up my pants legs.
When the blender stopped,
My mother howled for us to sit.
Seven of us at the table, all of us quiet,
None of us with prayer,
None of us with anything to say,
And the poor turkey, just out
Of the oven and throwing off heat
From under its sizzling wings.

Sit straight! mother scolded.
Eat! stepfather spat.
This was family, this was Thanksgiving.
The turkey moaned when
The carving knife went in.

CATHOLIC EDUCATION

I stood in the wastebasket
In third grade,
In spring
When blossoms
Sailed outside the classroom window
Like kites I thought,
Like pretty litter...

How did I get there?
I can't recall
Except Sister Guadalupe
Pointed her clicker—
Chirp from the stone
In her heart,
Chirp that you're worthless,
Chirp that could clear
Wax from a dirty ear.

Jesus was nailed
To the wall,
The Pope,
President Kennedy,
Their eyes following
As I walked
To the corner.
My classmates,
Pencils working
At math problems,
Were indifferent to me—
What had I done?

I was stepping
Into the wastebasket,
Left foot first,
When I saw a crayon,
Periwinkle,
On the polished floor.
I picked it up
And sniffed its blunt tip.
I began to think
That maybe colors
Had different flavors,
Like red was pomegranate,
Yellow lemon,
Brown frijoles smeared
On a dinner plate.

Since I was in the corner
I had only to reach
Arms length,
One foot out the wastebasket
To sharpen the crayon.
Three cranks
And it snapped.
I peered into the hole
Of the sharpener—
Part of the crayon,
Snug as a bullet.

I dragged my eyes upward.
Jesus was eying me,
The Pope,
President Kennedy
Dead two years later,
With a little hole in his neck
Where a pretty crayon could fit.

I was only ten,
Garbage from the look
Of things, the blossoms
No longer parading
Past our classroom window.
My classmates were
Doing fractions,
And I knew
Numbers were going
To get smaller
And smaller,
Until nothing was left,
Until we kids no longer counted.

I feared Sister Guadalupe's clicker.
I feared Jesus on the wall,
His eyes were sorrowful, his halo
An untouchable gold,
And his four bodily wounds
Small enough to fit
The darkest crayons.
I could give the crayons
A turn and break them off,
And break off
With Jesus, Nordic
At the time—his eyes
Were periwinkle
But right then blood red
In his angry stare.

Going Natural

The pharmacist with a polished head,
With the ears of an elephant,
With the Mason emblem on his lapel,
Roared, What?

Prophylactics, I stuttered,
My eyes raised and whispering, You know…
The fellow didn't know
And clicked his ballpoint pen a dozen times,
Which I counted as twelve seconds of exquisite masturbation.
I turned to assess the line behind me.
At the end, a lady rifling through a furry coin purse,
And suddenly I thought of pussy,
A small dent, of money well spent—
God, the red of a broken hymen all over my face.
Again, I whispered, Prophylactics,
To which he hollered, Speak up!
More hymen on my face,
More blood. Finally, the woman
With a puss, I mean purse,
Looked up and said, John, the boy wants rubbers.

I left the pharmacy, wiser by one day,
And sat in the park feeding potato chips to frenzied carp,
Their gaping mouths like smelly kisses—
One girl carp climbed out of the pond
And nearly followed me home.

I took off my shoes. I wiggled my toes
And walked naturally on the grass,

A sensation that had me shutting my eyes in pleasure.
And the prophylactics? I threw all
But one away. That lucky fellow
Stayed in my wallet,
Just in case, its round shape tooled naturally
By my sitting, rising, and sitting again.

AN UNCLE IN ASSISTED LIVING

He saluted the flag, waved
To a twin-engine P-42 lifting from Chandler Field.
He brought down birds with BB guns—
It was all in good fun, he and Eddie Bond
Belly flopping in the grass at the beginning
Of the 1940s. He made his own kind of war—
The bullfrogs didn't stand a chance.

After the war, it was all a lie.
The commies never came,
Not much came except two wives
Who drove off with his cars—
One returned for the stackable washer and dryer.

He coughs, and coughs, and coughs.
His eyes seep. A magician,
He pulls a handkerchief from his sleeve.

At eighty-eight, every day hurts.
He plays tug-of-war with the bright tennis balls
On the feet of his walker. In the garden,
The birds he brought down have resurrected themselves.
The bullfrogs regroup in ditches.
Still, he has no regrets. The Nazis went up in smoke,
The commie came down with the wall.
What else? he thinks, water in his eyes.
What else? he complains. He smiles—
His teeth, like furniture, went with the house.

CAMPESINO

Spring '93, I'm five time zones from my country
And hacking soldier-straight weeds—
I'm captain of their destruction. But the army
Of weeds keeps advancing, day after day.
I was a math teacher in Mexico,
But now I'm a number squeezed into a white van,
The stars blue as my life at 5:30 in the morning.
But don't feel sorry. I have my hands and back,
My face dark as a penny in a child's palm.
I walk a straight row. My lean shadow keeps up.
But look at the circling seagulls,
Landlocked with no way home.

If there's work, I hoe nine hours in the beet fields,
Sometimes with my *primo* in the next row,
Sometimes alone. You would be crazy
To open your mouth—the wind and dust…
In a year, my face will be tooled like my wallet,
Dark and creased. Over the clods,
I sing to myself, or whistle like a parrot.
I practice English—
Waffles, no good tire, nice to meet you.

In the fields, I stop when
The *patron* on the tractor path says stop.
I pound sand from a boot like an hour glass.
Time pours forever and forever.
Tomorrow I start again. I'll chop at the earth
But it won't bleed under my hoe.
I'll chop, sweat, and think in English—
Toaster, thread, seagulls find a way home.

CHRISTMAS IN EAST LOS ANGELES

In the front yard manger
Baby Jesus gripped a plastic rattle
And wore a Pamper a size too large.
The Christmas lights dangled like fruit
Over His glorious head.

The Three Kings hovered over the Prince of Peace.
The donkey smiled, the two lambs smiled,
The camel fallen on its side
Was smirking.

Mary and Joseph...
I looked up at the front window.
A woman worked a dishcloth over the glass,
Her own hair crowned with yellow light.
I made out a child running behind her.

On the trellis
Chili-shaped Christmas lights glowed.
The chicken in the yard blinked near the rose bush,
The family's Christmas soup?

I slid my hands into my pockets.
Someone was singing,
Someone was sweeping a porch.
Even I, a passerby, a sojourner,
A man who may end up in a diaper,
Breathed a halo into the morning air.
Peace comes to us all.

BREAD & BUTTER

The ant brings home a log,
The jay a many-legged insect dead of fright,
The mole a turnip,
The cat a mouse minus its face...

If you're a breadwinner,
Something must be brought through the front door,
Or why does the table exist
If not for a ham topped with a rung of canned pineapple?
Why does the chair exist if not for our squirming bottoms?
Why do the mouth and eyes water
At the splitting of a watermelon?

I refold my wax paper
And shove it into my back pocket.
The plastic water bottle I refill at the faucet.
My work? Stationed at my lathe,
I spin out wooden legs,
Sometimes an arm, one time a pianist's finger.

At the end of the day
I wash in the washroom
And bring home bags of groceries,
The tambourine of coins in my pocket
For the Pakistani ice cream truck.
I work with wood,
Could be said I'm made of wood.
I own what I own. The bank can't knock at my door.
Is that the truest thing I'll say before sleep?

Evenings on the porch, I can spit on my lawn,
Or sail my truck right onto it.
I don't have to visit a lake—
The rotating sprinkler cools my neck
And pleases my offspring,
All sturdy as bowling pins.
My job is to make wooden legs,
Tall ones and short ones,
Some of pine, others of hardheaded maple.
You'd be surprised how hundreds
Of legs get lopped off by trains.

My neighbor does art—
Can't say he's good, can't say that he's bad.
But he's skinny as a rake,
His belt is on its last notch,
And his blood is for sale—
This is how much he needs money.
I'll tell you this: there's more paint on his shirt
Than that canvas stretched to hollering.

This neighbor—artist, I guess—could learn from the ant.
He could learn from the jay and the mole,
From the cat as well—or even me, daddy on the porch.
I pull a wood shaving from my hair,
A little natural curl, and slip it on my daughter's thumb.

WHAT YOU MIGHT EXPECT

On the park bench
Henry James turns the page of a travelogue—
The tired master is eating the last of a puffy croissant
Near the border of Italy and France.
A crumb has attached
Itself to his beard—oh, the faux pas
Of greeting Madame du Coudray,
With his top hat coming off,
He bows like a bending willow.

The horror, Mr. James thinks later,
When he touches his chin
And finds crumbs in his beard,
Crumbs verified in the reflection
From the tobacconist's shop window—
The pipes were set in a row.

If you're a poet on a public bench,
You might expect this,
A crumb or two on your stubbly face
At an hour when everything has been eaten.
You don't have much to do—
The smoldering cigarette is snuffed out
Under your boot. Behind you,
Near the slide shiny as a spoon,
A child is pouring sand
Through his fists like an hourglass.

Birds in the trees, some by the dry fountain…
The smallest bird is waiting to pick up after you.

What Did You Expect?

The collie didn't come when called,
And a cloud descended, stripping away
Every red apple on the neighbor's tree.
The weather vane failed to announce
A promised wind. The climate changed—
One day hot, the other day snow
On the roofs of your shoulders.
The gopher closed his hatch,
Roots like dental floss between
His front teeth. He wasn't involved,
And neither was the skunk nor skunk's friend,
The possum in pajamas.
The deer came down from the hills,
Looked around, and went back
Into the hills. Al Gore hitched up his pants
And called it Global Warming.
A movie was made, awards given out.
Another cloud buckled
And stripped away the pears,
The Buddha of all fruits.

When you touch a rose, the petals fall off—
You discover they were real after all.
When you call "Kitty, Kitty, Kitty"
To a red fox, that gamey creature spits
And scurries away. At a distance,
It looks back, eyes narrow
As hatchets, and growls, Bite Me, Fucker.
It spurts urine to remind himself
Where not to go.

Gary Soto began as a poet in the early 1970s, but has enjoyed critical and commercial success in all genres and for all ages. His thirty-plus books have sold over four million copies. His best-known works include *Living Up the Street, A Summer Life, Buried Onions, The Afterlife,* and *New and Selected Poems,* a finalist for the 1995 National Book Award. The Gary Soto Literary Museum is located at Fresno City College. He lives in Berkeley, California.

CPSIA information can be obtained
at www.ICGtesting.com
Printed in the USA
FSOW02n0050270415
6690FS